MW00490227

Grief-Walking

Four Prayerful Steps to Healing After Loss

by
Linus Mundy

Sharon Kidd
Contributing Author

ONE
CARING
PLACE

Abbey Press

DEDICATION

To Mom, Anna B. Mundy

Library of Congress Catalog Number
98-71233

ISBN 0-87029-316-8

Printed in the United States of America

CONTENTS

Foreword: How This Book Can Help vii

Introduction: A Working Definition
   of *Grief-Walking*.................................1

Chapter I: How *Nature* Heals Grief...........7

Chapter II: How *Movement* Heals Grief ...17

Chapter III: How *Praying* Heals Grief......25

Chapter IV: How *Remembering*
   Heals Grief...33

Chapter V: How to *Pull It All Together*—
   and Grief-Walk Toward Healing............41

Appendix I: Why I Grief-Walk
   by Sharon Kidd..................................53

Appendix II: Meditations and
   Prayer-Starters for Your
   Grief-Walking Journeys.......................79

Bibliography 83

"*Above all, do not lose your desire to walk. Every day I walk myself into a state of well-being, and walk away from every illness. I have walked myself into my best thoughts, and I know of no thought so burdensome that one cannot walk away from it.*"

—Søren Kierkegaard

How This Book Can Help

This little book is based on several simple but important premises:

Premise One: We can't escape or walk away from grief; we walk *through* it. And walking—not running, not crawling—is the proper pace to be traveling.

Premise Two: Grief strikes at the "all of us"—not just at the "parts" of us. Grief strikes at our bodies, our minds, our spirits. It hits us from head to toe. It hits us heart and soul. It hits us inside and out. To come out of grief healed, we need to heal the whole, integrated

persons that we are. *Grief-Walking* is entirely
devoted to this kind of holistic, whole-person
healing exercise. It's intended to be a book to
help pull "all of you" together—at a time when
you may be feeling that everything has been
torn apart.

Premise Three: We walk differently after
we've experienced grief in our lives. Some of
this "whole new way of walking" is easier,
kinder, gentler. But some of it, certainly at
first, is going to be much more halting and
difficult, and we do well to recognize that.

Our hardest grief work, in fact, involves
rediscovering that *the world is still a safe place.*
For a long time after a loss, whether sudden or
expected, our worldview is changed. We're like
the soldier coming home from a far-away war.
Before the war, and as he was "marching off to
war," the soldier's worldview was smaller, safer.
After the war, he sees that it's a much larger
and far more dangerous world in which he
marches. He may not even trust family and

old friends anymore, at least for awhile.

When an elderly loved one dies, we come to the stark conclusion that a "permanent fixture" in our lives is not permanent after all. Our new logic tells us that what was once predictable isn't predictable anymore. *"I don't trust happiness anymore,"* goes the heart-rending line from the bereaved father in the movie *Tender Mercies.* After experiencing deep loss, we can relate to that.

To counter this new sense of uncertainty and unpredictability, we will work our way back to trust within this book, discovering together that there are places where we can still walk in safety, predictability, comfort, and trust. More than that, we will grief-walk together to places where we can remember gently, commune with God mystically, and come to healing more fully than we may have imagined possible.

Premise Four: Everyone's grief-walk will be different, everyone's situation is different, every path to healing is surely as different as one's fingerprints (or, in this case, one's footprints!) Don't be afraid to adapt the suggestions and directions contained here to meet your unique needs. After all, one size does *not* fit all—not in walking shoes, and not in grief-walking, either!

Let us begin our prayerful, healing, grief-walking journey together.

*Through this world of toil and snare,
If I falter, Lord, who cares?
Who with me my burden shares?
None but thee, dear Lord,
none but thee.*

—*"Just a Closer Walk with Thee"*

INTRODUCTION

A Working Definition of *Grief-Walking*

Several years ago, I wrote a little book called *Prayer-Walking: A Simple Path to Body-and-Soul Fitness* (Abbey Press). In that volume, I described prayer-walking as "exercise for the whole person: body, mind, and spirit."

This practice, or technique, which is sometimes called "walking meditation," has many degrees or levels of simplicity—or complexity—depending on one's needs, desires, and personality. As with many other physical/mental/spiritual exercises or disciplines, there are varying degrees of difficulty as well as devotion which may be applied to prayer-walking.

A year after the small, introductory volume on prayer-walking appeared, I was invited to produce a more detailed book on the subject, *The Complete Guide to Prayer-Walking* (Crossroad). In this latter book, I describe the various ranges or levels of practice within this wonderfully healing exercise called *prayer-walking*. I like to describe one level, one end of the spectrum, as "Huckleberry" prayer-walking. Using this technique, one simply, casually, informally wanders or saunters about—but with an agenda: a concentrated sense of prayerful intention, or God-mindfulness. For example: One steps outside and walks to the mailbox to get the day's mail—and to be in communion with God. This simple little errand or exercise is, in itself, prayer-walking. One's mind and heart are intentionally turned toward God in or by the process.

At the other end of the spectrum—what might be called a more advanced level—is a rather formal, structured, don't-miss-any-part-of-this technique. In a nutshell, it involves the combination and careful coordination of four basic components to make it effective:

- Breathing
- Counting
- Stepping
- Utterance

Pulled all together, and put in the simplest of terms, a sample 20-minute grief-walk, during which I am working through the death of a friend named Joe, might go something like this:

- I step outdoors and start walking at a comfortable pace.
- I begin to notice my breathing pattern.
- I count how many steps I take on my in-breath (probably 3 or 4).
- I count how many steps I take on my out-breath (probably 3 or 4).
- *In place of* the count on my in-breath—"1, 2, 3, 4"—I substitute the syllables of my utterance (prayer or mantra): "God-keep-you-Joe"...and then on my out-breath I do the same: I either *repeat* the same 3- or 4-syllable phrase *or* add another one, such as: "We'll-meet-a-gain."

I describe the methods and techniques, and how to coordinate them, in the pages that follow. I also invite you to find out more about grief-walking by reading some of the works cited in the Bibliography at the end of this book. For now, suffice it to say that the process is one of uniting body, mind, and spirit humbly before God, in and through the simple human activity of walking.

———✧✧✧———

"*Meet my psychiatrist*"
—Nature photographer Les Blacklock,
referring to the healing power of nature

CHAPTER ONE

How *Nature* Heals Grief

It takes us a lifetime to rediscover some of the truths we knew so well in childhood. Here's one of those truths, I believe: Playing in our own backyard, and getting dirty there, is good for us. The reason: there is something in the dirt we played in as children that provided an always-available, common-as-dirt miracle—as common as creation itself. It showed we were a part of something much bigger than we could possibly comprehend:

something that preceded us, and something that will succeed us, too.

In our adult lives, we continue to witness near and far the incredible wonder and power of nature in our lives. We see it in the world at large and in our everyday experiences. We cut our finger, see the blood, and feel the pain; two weeks later, there is hardly a trace of damage or hurt. On a Pacific island, a volcano erupts with devastating power and spews massive ash over hundreds of square miles. In our minds, we write off the entire area as a total, irrevocable loss. And then, months later, we read about the scene, and—to our astonishment—see pictures of green sprigs popping up everywhere and wildlife scurrying near and far in their revived habitat.

Nature restores. But exactly what is it in nature that restores? After the finger cut and the volcanic eruption, it is partly time, of course, that makes the healing difference. But what is happening during this time? Simple and totally reliable and natural things such as blood flow, oxygen, sunshine, rain, the nutrients inside us and in the soil beneath our feet, combine to bring about restoration. Indeed, nature packs power, possibility, unstoppability within itself, embracing all and everything.

Yes, while nature surrounds us with visions of all-pervasive death, it also surrounds us with visions of irrepressible life, cycle after cycle. By our close observing of nature, by paying attention, we see nature in all its brutality—and gentleness. We can witness lichens "eating" rocks, bones turning into soil, soil squeezing up sprigs of green growth. *And Nature invites us to participate—intimately—in a marvelous phe-*

nomenon we might simply call resurrection.

How do *we* participate? On one level, we can participate passively, unconsciously. We can simply "leave it to nature." Indeed, our imaginations often will soar simply by the visual pleasures we can experience through contact with the natural world. Psychologists contend that human well-being is fostered when our physical sur-roundings give us gentle, natural, moderate degrees of positive stimulation. As one nat-uralist puts it: "How can you improve upon the stimulation one receives upon discovering the first crocus of spring pok-ing through the remnants of winter's last snow? Or the rush of fond memories when sniffing the fragrance of an heirloom rose grown long ago?"

There's also a more consciously active way to participate with nature. To paraphrase an ancient Greek poet: "If you are hungry and have only three coins, buy one loaf of bread and two hyacinths." The voluntary way to participate in nature involves buying into nature's healing benefits by conscious, active participation. And that's what this little book is all about.

"Every time I go fishing, it takes me farther from the lake," says a reflective friend of mine, working through a painful loss. What he is saying to me is: "When I go fishing these days, I'm fishing for more than fish. I'm working out some things that are important in my life."

One of the things my friend is fishing for is answers. And even though he's gotten wise to the fact that there are no easy answers to the "Why" questions related to loss, he's spending time on a lot of the "What now?" questions.

We can choose to employ the power of nature for our healing from grief. But we need to be attentive. We can walk along the beach and do budget calculations for the corporation, or deliberate on what color to paint the porch next Saturday—or we can enter into the world of the powerful, pounding ocean waves and the eternal sand between our toes. Nature can be *just there*, like background music or scenery, or we can highlight it as foreground and visit it often, allowing it to be a counselor or therapist for us on the grief-healing journey. When we enter into the experience fully, nature can be an old friend to whom we take our troubles, a place we can go to with our collected—or scattered—thoughts.

One doesn't need to be a professional naturalist to gain the marvelous benefits nature has to offer. But, as Sharon Kidd reminds us in her Appendix to this book, *the people who do the best after suffering a loss are those who have an established connection with nature—or with God.* And my own contention is that the people who do *the very best* are those who have an established connection with both nature *and* God.

So, as we grief-walk, we need to pay attention to what nature is saying to us, but also to what God is saying to us—in our hearts, in our minds, in and through nature. Wrote Trappist monk Thomas Merton: "One has to be alone, under the sky, before everything falls into place and one finds [his or her] own place in the midst of it all. We have to have the humility to realize ourselves as part of nature. Denial of this results only in madness and cruelties."

We need to learn—firsthand, by seeing it, smelling it, touching it out there on the walking trail—that there is lots of decay and decline and death; but with all that, there are equal parts of miraculous restoration, rejuvenation, renewal, *resurrection!* And it's a resurrection we can count on as sure as people throughout the ages have counted on the coming of the new growing season after the dark days of winter.

A Grief-Walk With Dad
(Joseph Mundy, 1915-1985)

Step 1: A good, strong, "cleansing" breath as I step outdoors.

Step 2: A mental image of the kind, gentle giant of a man Dad was, and the walks we used to take around the house, looking at and talking about whatever we happened to see: a shutter that needed repair, the chill in the November air, how old we guessed a certain tree to be.

Step 3: Start walking; start counting; start conscious breathing and counting of breaths—keeping the image of Dad in my subconscious.

Step 4: Replace the counting with a meaningful utterance: "1-2-3-4" becomes "Thanks, God, For Dad."

———◈◈◈———

"Be leisurely, and act vigorously."
—Sam Keen

How *Movement* Heals Grief

A British writer quipped that the reason Americans invented the rocking chair was so that they could still be moving while they were sitting!

Admittedly, those of us in the U.S. are an efficient people, and we like to be on the go—even while we are relaxing, and even while we are praying! (I just came across a new book entitled *Sweat Your Prayers: Movement as Spiritual Practice* by Gabrielle Roth. Indeed, there are now many books which espouse the spiritual value of movement, "body prayer," walking meditation, healing through "muscle-motion.")

Herbert Benson, M.D., has become somewhat of a household name thanks to his studies of exercises combining word and movement. The creator of a technique known as the Relaxation Response, Benson heads the Mind/Body Medicine Institute at Harvard Medical School in Boston. In a study conducted with James Rippe, M.D., Benson showed that walking and praying together are more beneficial than either activity alone. The people in the study participated in a standard fitness walking program and focused their minds. Says Benson, "We found it was possible for them to elicit the relaxation response while exercising, and thus to get the benefit of both [relaxation and exercise] at once." In earlier studies, Benson discovered that prayer and meditation elevate one's mood and produce beneficial physiological effects, including slower heart rate, lower blood pressure, and key hormonal changes.

In an article in *Your Health* (October, 1995), Benson draws some conclusions: "Our subjects concentrated on their foot-fall, but the principle is the same as if they had been praying. Their focus brought on the relaxation response. They felt better after the walk than they would have just walking alone. They derived the same cardiovascular training but had a measurable boost in mood and a reduction in stress."

What are the implications for grief-walking? In times of bereavement, we are particularly vulnerable to stress and depression. In grief-walking, we can counter stress and depressed emotions by exercise. Further, one of the best things about walking exercise—as opposed to the more strenuous running or weight-lifting, for example—is that walking is not so closely associated with exercise as with a simple, non-threatening getting from here to there. And that means people will be more likely to pursue this method, no matter their level of physical conditioning. It is more ordinary, although its benefits clearly are anything but ordinary.

On an immediate level, grief-walking lets you know that, despite the loss of a loved one, you are still alive. I say this at some risk of being challenged, in that all of us have been taught so well to tend to the lives of others rather than our own. But what would our loved one want for us? What does God want for us? Life... *Vitality* (from *vita*, meaning life). Take a walk—a grief-walk, or any walk—and no sooner do you take a few steps than you know there is *life* in these muscles and bones of ours! Grief-walking tells us that our lives still matter; our lives still count; our bodies and hearts and souls are still to be nurtured and nourished and loved. Every faith tradition known to humankind teaches this. Now, after loss, and after in many cases months and months, if not years, of selfless care of another, it's time to be good to ourselves.

Grief-walking is about healthy grieving—about taking care and being well, or at least as well as one can be under trying circumstances. As Dr. Evelina Mendoza-Mabini writes in the foreword to *Grieving as a Woman* (Abbey Press): "During periods of intense grief, a person tends to neglect health habits such as good nutrition, exercise, hygiene, and rest, and thereby puts further stress on the body. It can be a vicious cycle." I suggest we walk our way out of that cycle.

Another healing facet of grief-walking is the simple fact that when one is walking, one is making a forward movement. This sends a very important—even if subconscious—message to the spirit. Any notion or symbol, especially a voluntary and repetitive one, of making "forward progress" at a time of grief is of critical importance. Further, the simple fact that walking means putting one foot in front of the other, and the simple fact that it is a repeated, and 100-percent predictable, process (What happens after this step? Another step, huh? And after that? Another step! Yes, but after that?? Another step.) within a world that has become, because of your loss, anything but predictable, is of immeasurable comfort and consolation and healing.

Grief-walking—forward movement—helps us heal: Step...by step...by step.

———◇◆◇———

*T*here is a path from grief to grace.
And it is best walked with Another.

CHAPTER THREE

How *Praying* Heals Grief

Do you know it's OK to pray for yourself? As a matter of fact, there may be no more important cause than this. After the death of someone you love greatly, pray for hope. Pray for the strength, the will, to get out of bed in the morning, the strength to find your way.

Author Elie Weisel says that when someone is suffering, and it is not you, it is more important to think of that person than to think of God. But what if it is you?

Some years ago a friend of mine was going through a loss, feeling lost and unsure of his next step in life. I, in my cocksure wisdom, quoted to my friend a well-known saying of Gandhi: "Whenever you are in doubt or when the self becomes too much with you, try the following expedient: Recall the face of the poorest and most helpless person you have ever seen and ask yourself if the step you contemplate will be of any use to that person...Then you will find your doubts and your self melting away."

What was my grieving friend's humble response? "I'm sorry, but the poorest, most helpless person I can think of right now is me." After a loss, in the midst of grief, it *is* you. And that's OK. It's time for you to pray for you. Do that in lots of ways— including on a grief-walk.

How will prayer help you? It will connect you with the greatest Source of solace, peace, and healing available to us: our God who wants us to be whole.

Does prayer really heal? Medical doctors are now taking a good look at the power of prayer to heal. As a matter of fact, 99 percent of doctors attending a 1997 meeting of the American Academy of Family Physicians agreed that "a patient's spiritual beliefs can be helpful in his or her medical treatment," and 58 percent said that they themselves actively sought out information on spirituality and healing.

Dr. Larry Dossey, former chief of staff at Medical City Dallas Hospital and former co-chair of the Panel on Mind/Body Interventions for the National Institutes of Health, is a leading proponent of the scientific credibility of prayer. The author of

Prayer Is Good Medicine, Dossey says there is lots of scientific evidence that prayer works. "More than 130 controlled laboratory studies show that prayer or a prayer-like state of compassion, empathy and love can bring about healthful changes in many types of living things...."

In his book *Timeless Healing,* Dr. Herbert Benson argues that humans are "wired for God," and that "our genes guarantee that we will bear faith and that our bodies will be soothed by faith. I have found that faith quiets the mind like no other form of belief, short-circuiting the nonproductive reasoning that so often consumes our thoughts."

And what did the subjects of Dr. Benson's studies choose when asked to select a word or phrase on which to focus their healing? Fully 80 percent chose something spiritual, such as "The Lord is my shepherd," "Hail Mary," or "Lord, Jesus Christ, have mercy on me." Most of us would call these phrases expressions of prayer.

Now comes the tough question for many pray-ers who are grieving a loss: What about those of us who prayed our hearts and souls out—and yet lost the one we so earnestly prayed for? One answer is that prayer, ultimately, is not something we do for the sake of *gain*—a physical healing, a miracle cure—but rather for the sake of *unity*. Prayer, after all, is about relationship. When we prayer-walk or grief-walk, we realize that God always walks with us. God walked with Adam and Eve in the garden, God walked among us in the person of Jesus. And we believe that God walks among us now in the Spirit, too.

The late Abraham Joshua Heschel sums it up: "Prayer is not a stratagem for occasional use, a refuge to resort to now and then. It is rather like an established residence for the innermost self. All things have a home; the bird has a nest, the fox has a hole, the bee has a hive. A soul without prayer is a soul without a home." When we go for a grief-walk, we invariably "come home" to a stronger, more intimate relationship with our loving God.

Go home! And walk there!

Sample Grief-Walk: "A Lamentation Walk" With the Lord

Step 1: Read Psalm 13, with its refrain: "How long, O Lord? Will you forget me forever? How long will you hide your face from me? How long must I bear pain in my soul, and have sorrow in my heart all day long?"

Step 2: Take a big, cleansing breath to get started.

Step 3: Start walking, keeping the Psalmist's lamentation (or your version of it) in mind.

Step 4: Count your steps on your in-breath, 1-2-3-4 (or 1-2-3, if more comfortable), and likewise on your out-breath.

Step 5: Substitute your own utterance or "lamentation" for the numbers; that is: "1-2-3-4" becomes: "How long, O Lord?"

Step 6: Keep repeating the above prayer, in rhythm with your steps and your breathing, for 20 minutes.

It is love that matters and lasts.
Remember love.

CHAPTER FOUR

How *Remembering* Heals Grief

Where shall we grief-walk? Among other places, down memory lane—as painful as that may be for us. For, as chaplain Betty Hopf says, "It is more painful to try to forget than to remember."

And so, as we grief-walk, we walk not only with God but with the very one we have loved and lost. Marcel Proust said it well: "You will not be cured, but one day—an idea that will horrify you now—this intolerable misfortune will become a blessed memory of a being who will never again leave you."

My mother, I know, will never again leave us. And today, on the anniversary of her death, I have just come back from a grief-walk honoring her life—and honoring the hurt, and the joy, I still feel when I think of her and her life. On my grief-walk I imagined she was there walking with me. Yes, it slowed me down (Mom was a slow walker in her later years, but not always so!), and I like that part.

Some lines of a poem by Emily Dickinson came to mind as I grief-walked with Mom:

> *I walked a mile with Pleasure,*
> *She chatted all the way.*
> *But left me none the wiser*
> *For all she had to say.*

I walked a mile with Sorrow
And never a word said she
But oh, the things I learned from her
When Sorrow walked with me.

I've had similar grief-walks with my
memories of the lives of other dear folks
I've lost in my life: Dad, and Patsy and Pat,
and so many others. And when I walk with
them, I walk with the essence of them,
which forever remains. It's their spirits, and
our love, that still and forever live. When I
walk with Dad, for instance, we still don't
say very much. And that's the way we both
like it.

It is right and good that those who
have walked before us be our walking
companions today. And we can choose
whether we want our walk with them to be
a consoling one, a whimsical one, or even a

confronting one, where we "step outside" with them and work out some unfinished business.

Memories are personal. Whether it's simply speaking, repeating the name of your beloved one, walking to or around a favorite place you used to share, the key is to make and preserve *connections*. Grief-walking helps you strengthen cherished connections with someone you have loved and continue to love. As grief writer Donna O'Toole teaches in her workshops: "Grieving our losses does not disconnect us from life but rather, like invisible threads, the losses of our lives weave life unto life." And as playwright Thornton Wilder concluded about memories of a loved one: "All that we know about those we have loved and lost is that they would wish us to remember them with a more intensified realization of their reality. What is essential does not die but clarifies."

What is essential? That which we must remember most: the love—undying, forever love—emulating the greatest love, God's love, as proclaimed to us with such power and conviction by the Psalmist:

> *The heavens are telling the glory of God;*
> *and the firmament proclaims his handiwork.*
> *Day to day pours forth speech,*
> *and night to night declares knowledge.*
> *There is no speech, nor are there words;*
> *their voice is not heard;*
> *yet their voice goes out through all the earth,*
> *and their words to the end of the world.*

—Psalm 19:1-4

Gratefulness is also essential—gratefulness for the love. Writes Buddhist monk Thich Nhat Hanh in his book about walking meditation, *The Long Road Turns to Joy:* "We who have two legs can easily practice walking meditation. We must not forget to be grateful. We walk for ourselves, and we walk for those who cannot walk. We walk for all living beings—past, present, and future."

———◈◈◈———

*P*eace can come—when we let go.

CHAPTER FIVE

How to Pull It All Together—and Grief-Walk Toward Healing

Just as there are no wrong ways to grief-walk, there are no perfectly right ways either—except the way that's right for you. But there are ways that seem to be proven by time and experience. This chapter will elaborate on the key concepts involved.

Keep in mind the words of writer Emilie Griffin, from her *The Reflective Executive*: "Visit the botanical gardens or a nearby nature trail. In your walk, be contemplative. If you don't know how to be contemplative, be what 'contemplative' means to you. Avoid making a production of it or sharpening your contemplative style. Instead, be a clumsy, not fully competent, awkward contemplative. Relax and let God do the work."

For me, so much of the technique of prayer-walking, and grief-walking, is related to *mindfulness*. What do I mean by this term? I mean "touching the ground of the present moment deeply," as Buddhist guide Thich Nhat Hanh describes it. "It is only when you realize that peace and happiness are available here in the present moment that you will be able to relax," says he. It is only when we realize that peace and happiness are available in the present moment that we will *heal*, I would add.

But what are the specific ways to do this? Just what is involved in a good grief-walk? We return to the four simple components first presented in the Introduction: Breathing, Counting, Stepping, Utterance. The trick is to get these components working in unison. It's simpler than it first appears, so fear not!

Breathing: What I am referring to here is *conscious* breathing, or awareness breathing. Although breathing is mostly an involuntary action, when we make it a voluntary one, or one we are consciously aware of, it takes on new significance. Says writer James Forest: "It comes to many as astonishing news that something as simple as attention to breathing has a central part to play in meditation and prayer."

Step one is to pay attention to your breathing. Breathing centers us, making us conscious, mindful, attentive, and connect-

ed to the Spirit (sometimes known as
anima, meaning *breath.*)

Counting: Count your steps as you
breathe in, and then count your steps as
you breathe out. Counting gives cadence,
tempo, rhythm, measure, the beat to our
walk. (The counting becomes transparent
after a bit—just as the notes of a musical
composition disappear after a while, and all
we hear is sheer *music!)*

Stepping: This is the "physical mantra,"
as someone described it. Its central func-
tion, of course, is simply to give us forward
movement, but it also brings us a sense of
rhythm, cadence, and harmony. Our steps,
one after the other, so simple and so predictable, are like the easy to-and-fro of the
schoolyard swing, the soothing back-and-

forth of the baby cradle or rocking chair, the joyful row-row-row your boat of the childhood song.

Utterance: This is the communication or message or prayer/meditation portion of our prayerful, healing exercise. With this component of our grief-walk, there are as many options as there are footprints! One thing is central here: Make sure the utterance or meditation means something to you personally.

If it's a repeated phrase, a mantra, make it one that is expressive and personal to you. Examples might include: the name of the person whose loss you are grieving, or a traditional phrase or brief prayer from your faith tradition—one that is comforting, consoling, reassuring, such as "My Jesus, Mercy," "Thy will be done," "God rest his/her Soul," or "Stay with me, God."

After getting comfortable with the matching up of your breathing and your stepping—and you do this by counting—it's time to pay attention to this utterance, a key component that perhaps more than any other makes prayer-walking *prayer*-walking or grief-walking *grief*-walking. Some would call this component the *mantra*; in some Christian traditions it is known as an *aspiration*. I think that's a very good word for it. An *aspiration* is typically a short formalized prayer of about a dozen words. Its purpose is to help one maintain a spirit of recollection in God's presence during the day. The word, appropriately, comes from the Latin *aspirare:* "to breathe upon."

The repeated word, phrase, or meditation needs to be as individual as I am, as you are, as the day is. When my mother was dying, my repeated prayer-walk was a prayer for her, for me, for our whole family and community of friends who were seeing a beautiful woman leave this life. It was the familiar prayer from Psalm 91:5, a "night prayer" chanted the world over in the Liturgy of the Hours: "You will not fear the terror of the night." I not only repeated those very words, I reflected on them and some of the other beautiful and reassuring words from Psalm 91, especially "With long life I will satisfy them."

Another time, when for months on end I grieved a change in my life, my chosen prayer as I walked was simply: "Lead...me...on." The words were taken from John Henry Newman's dramatic poem, "Lead, Kindly Light."

Today my favorite healing prayer is:

"God...loves" (in the drawn-out, four-beat and four-step rhythm of 1-2-3-4...1-2-3-4: "Go-o-o-d....Lo-o-o-ves"). Once I get into the rhythm of my walk, I often find myself moving from an everyday consciousness of things going on around me to a whole different realm—a realm where time stops and where true freedom, God's healing and peace, sets in.

—————✦———

My preferred grief-walking style involves the rhythmic repetition of an utterance. But there are other ways to grief-walk.

In *Walking a Sacred Path: Rediscovering the Labyrinth as a Spiritual Tool* (see Bibliography), Dr. Lauren Artress offers four options to pursue on a prayer-walk/grief-walk. Each revolves around a meditation rather than an utterance:

1. The Path of Image: Following the memories, dreams, or image that one's mind or imagination brings forward.

2. The Path of Silence: A centering, quieting-down approach, where the walker moves into the present moment, opening up heart and mind, all the while emptying heart and mind of the commotion of the outer world.

3. The Path of Prayer: In this method, one recites a traditional prayer, Scripture verse, line of poetry, or original prayer. This need not be in the repeated, rhythmic pattern as described above—but it could be, if you desire.

4. The Path of Questioning: On this path, the walker seeks an answer to a question, all the while knowing that the perfect solution or answer may not be found on the walk, but that possibilities are explored

more deeply and prayerfully through the process.

There are other elements to consider including in your own grief-walk. For example: Grief forces us to view the familiar with new eyes. We can let nature supply healing images as we participate in the inherent creativity.

Thus, as we grief-walk, we may conjure up untold images of nature, each representing an aspect of our personal grief journey. We may use—as I recently saw in a wonderful children's book on grief—such provocative natural images as "The Ocean of Loneliness," "The Cave of Fear," "The Winds of Anger," "The Guilt Swamp," "Diving Deep Into Our Memories."

It behooves us to pay attention to *where* we grief-walk. When I want to do some healing grief-walking concerning my dad,

for example, it's helpful for me to go walking in a field. This was his world: tall grass,
stubble, outdoor sights and smells. I'm
back in his world, with him again—at least
for a while. I know I can't stay there—it
wouldn't be healthy to try to stay too
long—but for awhile it is good, and life is
OK. Scratch that; … and life is *great,*
because we can remember yesterday while
also appreciating today—and awaiting
tomorrow with hope.

Life is right there in front of us. Let us
walk it, step by step, "while we have the
light."

"*What our prayer-walk can teach us, really, is that it's all holy ground we walk on—whether that ground is in the laundry room, in the boardroom, or under the roomy skies.*"

— "Taking a Prayer-Walk,"
an Abbey Press *PrayerNote*

Why I Grief-Walk
by Sharon Kidd

A Personal Story of Loss

I have a confession to make. Three years ago I was a confirmed indoor person. You might even say I was a bookworm. I sold books as a career, read books for relaxation, and my only sport was hunting for another good book. I still love books, but when I started to experience inner healing while hiking in the spring of 1995, one of my favorite books became *Hiking*

Kentucky (see Bibliography).

The story of my conversion to a passion for the forests and fresh air began with three tragedies. Those three tragedies have taken me to a turn in my life journey that has brought more inner peace and fulfillment than I could ever have imagined.

Married at the age of 19, I chose to be a full-time wife and mother as my career. Motherhood was a calling that I took seriously, and I saw my children as gifts from God, to be nurtured and directed to have a strong sense of self and a strong realization of God's presence in their lives.

First came my son Bobby. Two years later, after a troubled pregnancy, my second son, Christopher, died after surviving for one day following a breech birth. I was devastated by the loss, but I was advised, as were all bereaved mothers at that time, to get on with life and try to forget about the death of my baby. I did my best to push down the feelings of grief and to put aside any need to talk about the tragedy I had experienced. After another year, and a successful pregnancy, my daughter Kristi was born. I felt my family was complete and I settled down to being a mother, wife, and part-time student at a local college.

When my children were in high school, my best friend, Mary Ellison, and I decided to buy a Christian Bookstore that was for sale. I would manage it and she would take care of the finances. I was scared because I had never worked outside of my home. But the bookstore soon became a blessing to both of our families as we learned the art of retailing, and we hired Mary's niece, Amy, and my daughter, Kristi, and son, Bobby, as after-school clerks.

A second tragedy occurred on a rainy Thursday, in June of 1992. After waiting for 30 minutes for Amy to arrive at our early morning employee meeting, Mary received a call from the hospital. Amy had been in a head-on collision on the way to work and was in critical condition in the emergency room. After a mad dash to the hospital, an emergency helicopter ride to a hospital in Knoxville, Tennessee, and three agonizing days of uncertainty and waiting, Amy was pronounced brain dead and taken off life support. Mary's family was reeling with grief. I helplessly watched as they suffered intensely.

It seemed that I could sense Amy asking me to please help her family. The idea of a grief support group came to me. I discussed it with my pastor, Terry Lester, and he introduced me to the chaplain at a neighboring hospital. Chaplain Wayne Sibley and I developed six sessions for the support group, and invited anyone in the community to come.

The 16 people who attended, I'm happy to say, found great healing and encouragement in meeting together. Twice a year we offered the support group, and had between 15 and 25 people in each session. In 1994, we invited a professor from the college I had attended to join our team. Connie Howard became the third facilitator and we were very grateful for her help.

Not long after Connie joined our team, another tragedy touched the bookstore, as well as the whole community. Becky Greer had been a close friend for about 10 years. We had become especially close after her son Stephen died of leukemia at the age of 5. When her other three children were all in school, and she wanted to find a job, she started working part-time at our bookstore. In January of 1995, in a terrible tragedy at her home, her three children were shot and killed. Gam Greer, her husband and the children's father, was injured, and Becky had escaped by running for help. The tragedy devastated Becky and Gam, and the whole community was in shock.

I began to spend a lot of time with the Greer family and Mary's family, as well as with other families in the support group. I found myself becoming exhausted physically, emotionally, and spiritually. The suppressed grief for my son Christopher began to explode out of my subconscious, and my concern for Becky Greer's survival haunted me continually. I began to experience some physical symptoms of grief trauma and realized I needed to begin to actively deal with my stress.

Spiritual trauma followed. I felt betrayed by God. How could God allow such pain and devastation to families who loved him? I conveyed through prayer to God that he was no longer my friend and that I could never trust him again.

My colleague Connie, from Cumberland College, suggested that I try to spend some time away from my work and do some hiking. I also decided to go to a grief counselor, and found myself talking out deep feelings of grief for my son Christopher as well as for Amy, Kami, Todd, and Buzzy. Since there is a retreat center 20 minutes from my home, I planned to spend a day retreat there with three friends, walking in the Daniel Boone National Forest. The results were nothing short of remarkable and replenishing.

God Speaks Through Nature

I have always loved trees. In fact, they are all around my house. But I never felt their full energy until I went on that first hike at cleftRock retreat center the spring after the first winter of the Greer children's deaths. Director Bob Larkey took us into the deep woods surrounding cleftRock. The trees towered over us and I felt small in the scheme of things. We found an old cabin in which a family had been born, lived, and died. It had been abandoned for many years, but there were memories of the family still in the old house. I began to see that other generations had also suffered. Bob showed us the wildflowers hidden beneath the leaves, the ferns and delicate plants growing up through the rocks. I thought about inner strength that enables people to withstand harsh conditions and thrive even in a situation as hard as the Greers'. We walked to a hidden spring and were delighted to see it bubble out of the ground. Was there hidden strength I didn't know about that was there for me? Even the air seemed green, and the smell of the forest was intoxicating. I felt like a musty old house that had just been opened up to air out. I felt my soul stretch and sing with the birds that were beginning to build their nests all around us.

We climbed and sat on an enormous rock that held us all and didn't seem to mind the weight. I felt guilty for having such a renewing day when my friends had lost their whole existence. There seemed to be a strong message in the spring breeze that day, and it was telling me that there is life after death. Death isn't the end of relationships. Love never dies.

Then came a big challenge. Nathan Howard, a friend of my daughter and an employee at our store, offered to take Mary and me to a trail he enjoyed. We packed a lunch, and Nathan took his new rappelling equipment just in case we came upon a big cliff that needed climbers. The trail went down in the woods, over a little wooden bridge, and curled around a shallow stream that bubbled over rocks and roots. There was a quiet rippling sound of the water as we walked single file, helping each other up steep inclines, down slippery rocks, under a hanging precipice; we followed the trail until we found what we had been looking for. Hidden deep in the woods and cutting out the rocks, the stream became a beautiful waterfall. At the foot of the falls was an opening in the forest and big rocks to walk on until you could almost get under the rushing water.

This was the cliff where we set up the ropes, and Nathan taught us to rappel. I leaned back on the ropes that were securely tied to a tree and to my belt. The ropes gently dropped me to the ground. I wondered if I could ever again trust God like I trusted that rope.

I used to. I used to think I could ask God for anything and God would do it. But evil came into our lives and it took seven precious souls from us, and I wondered where God was when those tragedies happened.

During the summer, I continued to hover over Becky, and let my anger at God and life rage. I let go of most of my responsibilities at church, and I stopped praying. I had prayed for years before the tragedy for the one who had pulled the trigger in Becky's home, and it seemed God hadn't heard at all.

In September, I went to Callaway Gardens in Georgia, and was privileged to hike in those beautiful woods. On the first hike, the forest was very dark. It had been raining, and the clouds were rapidly moving with the shifting wind. I was walking behind the others on the trail, not really paying attention to the leader, when I suddenly looked to my left. Through the damp green air came several streams of exquisite sunlight. The light was piercing through the darkness of the forest. It was breathtaking. God seemed to be speaking through the beams of light. The light was saying that God would break through my darkness, that God knew right where I was, that God's light would find me and find

Becky. I began to make peace with God that day in the woods. I finally asked God once again for help. I joined a group of friends who were praying for Becky's healing.

The light did break through during the first week of February, 1996. In the darkest days of Becky's depression, God began to show her that he still existed by occurrences that could only be explained by God's intervention. Becky began to pay attention when a phone call from a stranger made her realize that another person also had multiple grief and was surviving. Rosemary Smith began calling Becky every day and became a lifeline for her. Each day brought gifts from different sources: a letter, a visit, a painting, a pair of her daughter's earrings that were found, and more stories of other grief survivors. Becky began to see a "pinpoint of light."

Maybe there was a God, and if so, a heaven. If there was a heaven, then her children were definitely there, safely watching her and waiting for her.

A miracle of healing began taking place in her soul. She began to pull out of her deep depression. God had answered our prayers for her in a dramatic way. But that made me even angrier at God. Why would God answer that prayer and fail to answer the ones we had prayed for the person who had fired the gun on the day of the tragedy?

The answer to that question came in a walk on a cold, snowy day a few weeks later. The snow came hard and deep. The road was hidden from view by the white drifts. It occurred to me that my questions needed the same patience I had for the melting snow. The road was only hidden for a while, like the answers to my questions.

I had confidence that the road was still there under the snow, and I began also to have confidence that there would be answers to my questions. The answers would be uncovered for me when I arrived in heaven. What I am seeing now is the beautiful evidence of God's compassion and care for Becky and Gam, in the middle of their Winter of Grief. That love is constant no matter what evil touches our lives. God is constantly with us, and was even with them on the day of their tragedy, holding them and carrying them through those awful first days of trauma. God was with the three children and was also carrying them to their heavenly home.

The Greers are moving steadily through their grief. Becky is doing some writing and some speaking about the way God has been revealed and shown to be faithful to her in the last three years. Gam is coaching, running, and riding his mountain bike, and they both work in the gardens around their home. Gam told me back in the summer that of all the hurting people he had met since the deaths of his children, the ones who were recuperating were the ones that had some connection with nature, through gardening, hiking, fishing, farming, or boating. He has felt the healing touch of God through nature.

Therapeutic Hiking

In the spring of 1995, I had gone on several hikes sponsored by the Forestry Service. On one of them I renewed an acquaintance with the trail guide, Lynn

White. She is a biology teacher and had been hired to talk about the wildflowers and other plants on our spring hike. Lynn and I had a common bond besides a love of hiking: She had also been touched by grief.

About 12 years before, her husband Jerry had died suddenly, and left her as a young widow with a 5-year-old son. After the hike, I approached Lynn about joining our support-group team to help us develop some therapeutic hikes for our group members. I told her about the healing I was finding through walking in the forest. She told me about her work in the forests after Jerry's death. She had accepted a job of finding microbes in a swamp and found it a wonderful place to cry and get angry and work until she was too tired to work anymore. Her healing also came in nature.

She accepted my offer, and that spring we took our first group on the Therapeutic Hike.

Lynn taught us to see the life all around us that we often walk past and take for granted. The subtle colors of the wildflowers often hid them from first glance. We had to look closely at the underbrush along the paths we walked to find the treasures of the wildflowers. I learned much from those delicate teachers of truth. They were very predictable and punctual. I found the Hepatica flowers in late March a sure sign that Spring was coming. The Trillium jumped out in April, and in May the Solomon's Seal and Dwarf Iris bloomed on my birthday. The Yellow Wood Sorrel and Whorled Loosestrife appeared in June and July. Later, in the early fall, the Astor and Small Wood Sunflower made a showing.

They could always be counted on, and they expressed the character of their Creator. God could always be counted on; God's ways are constant and dependable. I thought of God every time I saw a new flower appear.

In the forest the seasons came and, with them, death came to the flowers, trees, and animals. It was all part of the life process. I saw it happen as I walked the same path for several years. The forest accepted death, and grew from it, and was still beautiful and alive. God was teaching me through the seasons and the life cycle of the forest that death is an inevitable part of life. I learned to accept that truth.

Lynn also taught us about the trees in the forest. The trees shared lessons of inner strength. We saw trees growing out of rocks, their roots piercing through the cracks, reaching down to find water. We realized people were as strong as trees and could find hope even on a rock-like place. We found several wounded trees with large chunks taken out of their sides. They were still alive, surviving and healing as the bark slowly covered the amputation with new growth. We learned that people, like trees, are survivors. Many traumas in life can wound our souls and try to cripple our spirits, but it's our choice how we react to them. We can be chronic sufferers, or we can grow through our pain and become persistent survivors.

As Lynn and I talked about the nature facts she would teach, we found analogies to grief that became meditations and discussion starters for our gatherings at the end of the hikes. As we would have a drink of spring water and a slice of bread at the end of our journey, we found our shared insights from nature's lessons encouraging, and we found truths that we could take back with us to our daily lives.

One of my fellow hikers pointed out that just as we approach a steep part of the mountain and have to pace ourselves to get to the top, we have to pace ourselves during the difficult times in life, one step at a time. We need to help each other along the way with a helping hand over a fallen tree, or a steadying arm as we ford the slippery rocks of a swollen creek. We need each other to make it through life's journey. We need a sympathetic ear to listen to our pain as well as our joys, a strong shoulder to lean on when the way gets tough, a hand to hold as darkness seems to hide the path from view. Those with whom we choose to walk our path become God's way of expressing divine presence to us. God speaks to us through the companionship of other people as well as through the beauty of nature.

Linked to Eternity

Since I began hiking three years ago, I have tried to analyze the healing I have found in the forests and trails around my community. Several writers have offered insights that make sense. Linus Mundy wrote in *Prayer-Walking* that the phrase "communing with nature" suggests that when we make ourselves available to nature, nature makes itself available to us. And God is there for the asking.

In *The Toughest Days of Grief,* Meg Woodson writes that nature makes us feel alive again. It could be because more sunlight enters our eyes and makes us less prone to depression. It could be because the more we exercise, the more mood elevating chemicals, called *endorphins,* enter our bloodstream. It could be that we begin to reflect nature's mood. Woodson also suggests it has to do with beauty, and in pleasing us in so many ways, nature soothes our displeasure. She challenges us to delight ourselves with nature, and to absorb nature and its beauty. Nature reflects the ultimate beauty of God, and when we are so angry at God that we won't communicate, God will speak to us in another way: through creation.

Nature is a language of God. It speaks of God's love and care of all of creation. It puts life and death into eternal perspective. The forest is linked to eternity through the seasons' brilliant and predictable changes. I feel linked to eternity every time I walk there. I feel like time stands still and the mountains and trees, which have watched generation after generation walk under their sheltering shadows, are watching me. I feel them smiling as they watch me struggle with the questions of life and death, knowing that if I wear the questions out and release myself to the answers, some hidden and some revealed, I will join them in their ancient wisdom. Every time I enter the other world of the forests, I anticipate a plant, or rock, or animal that will reach out for my attention. As I meditate on its beauty and look for a message hidden in its being, God does the inner work of meeting the need I carry within me.

Phillip Keller writes in *Reflections on Nature,* "If we but take the time to pause and wonder, we shall see the beauty of our

Father's character etched upon every blade of grass and satin petal blowing in the wind. Beyond this gentle glory all around there stands serene and strong the wonder of His word to us. 'I have loved you with an everlasting love!' Oh, to rest our souls on this sure word!"

*T*his and only this:
Only do the right thing and love goodness
and walk humbly with your God

—Micah 6:8

Meditations and Prayer-Starters for Your Grief-Walking Journeys

Take one of these prayers with you, in your heart, as you grief-walk. Or let these prayers and prayer-starters inspire your own individual prayer as you walk the journey to healing with God at your side.

GRIEF HURTS. Dear God, no one told me I could hurt this much. I now know my life can never be the same again. Can it still be OK? You promised it would be better than just OK when you said, "I have come that you may have life—and have it to the full." I'm not feeling full right now; in fact, I'm feeling empty. I don't even want a full life right now. I just want a life. Show me the way to go from here, I pray.

I'M SCARED. Dear God, can you put an end to my fear? You told us not to worry about tomorrow; to be like the birds who have no concern about tomorrow, but scurry for today's food and drink...and song. I sometimes fear I won't find the nourishment even for today's hunger and thirst, much less ever sing again.

JUST TO TRUST AGAIN. Dear God, I can't seem to trust life, trust happiness anymore. And I worry I never will. Today I need to ponder and listen to those simple, all-trusting words of the mystic Julian of

Norwich: "And all shall be well, and all shall be well, and all manner of thing shall be well."

TAKING MY TIME. Dear Lord, I'm not getting over this loss as quickly as some seem to think I should. Please help me to recover at the pace that you see fit. Part of me wants to just get over this as quickly as possible—but another part of me says that if I get over this, I will be betraying the love of the one I've lost. Teach me, Lord, that in time I can be well again and still honor deeply the one I love so much.

ANCIENT CELTIC PRAYER

Be thou a bright flame before me,
Be thou a guiding star above me,
Be thou a smooth path below me,
And a kindly shepherd behind me,
Today, tonight, and forever.

———◦◦◦◦———

I find you, Lord, in all things,
in all my fellow creatures, pulsing with your life;
as a tiny seed you sleep in what is small
and in the vast you vastly yield yourself.
The wondrous game that power plays with things
is to move in such submission through the world:
groping in roots and growing thick in trunks
and in treetops like a rising from the dead.
—Rainer Maria Rilke

BIBLIOGRAPHY

The Complete Guide to Prayer-Walking: A Simple Path to Body-and-Soul Fitness by Linus Mundy, New York, New York, Crossroad Publishing Company, 1996.

Grief Therapy by Karen Katafiasz, St. Meinrad, Indiana, Abbey Press, 1995.

Hiking Kentucky by Darcy and Robert Folzenlogen, Littleton, Colorado, Willow Press, 1995.

The Long Road Turns to Joy: A Guide to Walking Meditation by Thich Nhat Hanh, Berkeley, California, Parallax Press, 1996.

Making It Through the Toughest Days of Grief by Meg Woodson, Grand Rapids, Michigan, Zondervan Publishing House, 1994.

Prayer-Walking: A Simple Path to Body-and-Soul Fitness by Linus Mundy, St. Meinrad, Indiana, Abbey Press, 1995.

Reflections on Nature by W. Phillip Keller, Milton Keynes, England, Nelson Word Ltd., 1993.

Walking a Sacred Path: Rediscovering the Labyrinth as a Spiritual Tool by Dr. Lauren Artress, New York, New York, Riverhead Books, 1995.

———◦◦◦◦———